.... *And She Said Unto Herself*

Seven Conversations Every Woman
Should Have Within Herself

———————

PASTOR VONYETT S. AKINS

Unless otherwise indicated, all Scripture quotations are from the Holy Bible, King James Version.

Published 2017
Printed in the United States of America
ISBN-13: 978-0692961131
ISBN-10: 0692961135

Cover Design by John Roberts/Kingdom Graphic Designs

For more information, please contact:
God's Gems Publishing
P.O. Box 2612
Warner Robins, GA 31099

Dedication

This book is dedicated to all my God's Gems:

To My Present Gems, I thank you for your continued belief in me and the anointing that is on my life. You have given me you as a platform while many just knew me as the "Apostle's Wife". You have been the first partaker of my own ministry and the first fruit of my labor. You have gotten the best out of me because you gave me all of you. You allow me to impart, share, correct, and mother you as I see fit and for that I Thank You.

To My Past Gems, what you did Then allows me to do what I'm doing Now. You saw then what I couldn't. I thank you for your push and what you always believed was in me and what would happen for me. Your time spent with me, your resources, and encouragement has helped to get me to this point, Thank You.

To My Future Gems, I thank God for you as well because I will touch far more people with my writings than I'll ever touch with my natural hands. If through these words I can help someone become a better woman, mother, or Woman of God then I've done a portion of what God has called me to.

Contents

Forward

By Apostle Daniel L. Akins

And She Said Within Herself......is a prophetic conversation that Pastor Von has had with the Holy Spirit and through her intimate time of communing she brings to us it's heart, mind, and wisdom. This book is wisdom crying in the streets, for those in the body of Christ as well as those that will apprehend this book filled with knowledge. This book is filled with strategies on how to win with the weapons of God's warfare to the pulling down of strong holds. There's not a boring page, it's captivating and stirring. You can sense the grace of a seasoned woman of God's handprint all over this writing. There is a prophetic element to this book that points you to clear directives and a practical element that will coach you into sobriety. What are you saying within yourself? If you are dying inwardly it will show outwardly. The fruit of your life is probably the fruit of your words. Death and life are in the power of the tongue and they that love it shall eat the fruit thereof. Let this book ignite a right conversation within you.

Every woman should have this book in her library, it will challenge you to agree with God and his word.

ACKNOWLEDGEMENTS

I first want to thank My Lord and Savior Jesus Christ for saving me and for touching my life. I'm blown away daily by his love for me and the fact that he's mindful of me.

To Mr. Daniel L. Akins, I thank you for your push and your encouragement. Your love, care, and concern for me has been endless. One of your heart's desire is for me to be and do everything that God has called me to. I'm so thankful and proud to call you Husband. Words can never express how grateful I am for You, you're certainly a cool drink in the heat of the battle. Thank you for loving me.

To Mommy, Sherlyne Duffy, I Love You Lady. Thank you for being whatever I needed you to be. A mother, a sister, a friend, a confidant, and most of all my truth bearer. To My Mother-and-law, Charlotte Akins, thank you. You have been a great supporter of our ministry. I'm grateful for

the part that you play in all of this. To the other half of my package deal, my Aunt, Francine Duffy, thank you for all you have done and continue to do for me and mine. You are the soft-spoken balance in my life, we love you Dutchess. To all my children, siblings, other family members, and in-laws thank you for your love and support. Much Love and Thanks to my God Parents Marboline Mullen and Leslie Mullen.

To Apostle Daniel L. Akins and More Sure Word Church, thank you for believing in me. For honoring the anointing that God has placed on my life and receiving it with an open heart and spirit. You are a great people to minister to, I love you.

A Special Thanks to John Roberts and Kingdom Graphics Designs for my book cover and website. Thank you to Alyssa Banks and ADesiCar Designs.

Introduction

There are so many challenges out there today. The media as well as social media is forever challenging us from one thing to another. They can all range from weight challenges to beauty challenges, and after we ourselves are challenged then we are encouraged to challenge those close to us and those that are around us. All those challenges are well and good. They prompt us to live healthier, increase our self-esteem, but I want to challenge you all to have a personal conversation with and within yourself. Yes, that's right a 7-day challenge to have a conversation with yourself. We have gotten so used to hearing from everyone else that we've not been able to benefit from what's on the inside of us, the power of our own voice. We have been so spoiled by waiting to hear what someone has to say that there have been seasons we have forfeited by not using and obeying our own voice. Many have gotten so lazy that we are no longer even encouraging ourselves. We won't even use our own voice to encourage and strengthen ourselves. We don't want to hear or speak to ourselves, so we wait on others to tell us what to do, what to think, where we should live, what feelings to have. We do none of these things on our own anymore because we are waiting on someone else to do that for us. So, we wait on the preacher, teacher, coach, and don't get me wrong all those people are great and needed. I just want us to get to a place that if none of those great people are in place or within our reach that we find a way to look within ourselves for the encouragement. There be many that are wandering through life wanting and looking for what's already on the inside of them. Not all of these conversations are good either, sometimes we must have some hard ones with ourselves. I'm convinced that if you never had a hard conversation with and or within yourself there's no way that we can properly receive one from someone else. That's why we do what we want, say what we want, and nobody better not dare say anything to us. We've got to get back to a time where we can speak to and judge ourselves. There are times I got to look at myself, me, not Pastor Von, not the Apostle's wife, but me. I must say to myself, "girl if you don't get yourself together", "that wasn't right", "what are you waiting for to go ahead and be great". It's not until after that that I'm able to say, "girl you can do it, you got this". I'm challenging someone today to begin to speak good words within yourself, encourage yourself, discipline yourself.

Conversation 1

There's Always Going To Be A Day After

Luke[7:11] *And it came to pass the day after, that he went into a city called Nain; and many of his disciples went with him, and much people.*

[12] Now when he came nigh to the gate of the city, behold, there was a dead man carried out, the only son of his mother, and she was a widow: and much people of the city was with her.

[13] And when the Lord saw her, he had compassion on her, and said unto her, Weep not.

[14] And he came and touched the bier: and they that bare him stood still. And he said, Young man, I say unto thee, Arise.

[15] And he that was dead sat up, and began to speak. And he delivered him to his mother.

[16] And there came a fear on all: and they glorified God, saying, That a great prophet is risen up among us; and, That God hath visited his people.

There is always going to be a day after. Yes, get that in your spirit and get that in your heart really good. There is always going to be a day after. The enemy always tries to play on the fact that this is your worst day ever and that we will never be able to get past this dark day or dark season in our lives. He knows that if we never get past the bad decision or the mistake we made then there goes our worth and value, and it came to pass the day after. We must know we are going to live past that evil day in our lives. We are going to live to face another day. Trouble doesn't last always. We are going to live past the divorce, we are going to live past our latest fall. We are going to live past our sons going to jail, we are going to live past our daughters getting pregnant while they are yet children themselves. I encourage you to have this conversation with yourself, say it within yourself, and mean it. Lift up your heads and rest in the fact there there's always going to be a day after. It may be a dark time now, you may be overwhelmed with situations and circumstances, but you got to know that there is going to be a day after this. Your season will change. Remember you thought that that last big thing was the worst thing ever. You thought your last big issue was the big thing, you thought surely it was going to take you out, but it eventually came to an end. Don't get stuck in a bad decision. Don't get stuck in your thinking that there is not going to be another day. Some will never establish their worth and value because they are stuck in a situation, an act, a decision, that happened 10 years ago. They are still defining themselves by an indiscretion that occurred 6 years, 6 months, 6 days ago. If you are going to go onward and upward, you are going to have to leave those situations and circumstances in the past and move on. The evil day will come to an end. There is going to be a day after the divorce, a day after you didn't get the promotion, a day after you got fired. While we are waiting on the next miracle or move of God we must know that there is going to be a day after. The text here is showing us that and makes it very clear. Jesus enters into a city called Nain, it's not only him. But it's also his disciples, and a large crowd that accompanied him as well. Now you really may not have to have this conversation with yourself if you've never had a private season or issue go public. You were not fortunate to be embarrassed in front of a few family members or a couple of coworkers, but you've experienced death in some areas right in front of leadership or in front of the whole entire town. What you went through was not able to be kept quiet or undercover. I mean an issue greater than the whole neighborhood seeing the Rent A Center truck back up to your house. The whole block saw your belongings being placed on the sidewalk, everybody saw your customized car on the back of the repo truck. These are some real-life issues, but I'm talking about a death in areas even greater than these. There's always going to be a day after. When it's one death after another. Her husband had already died. No doubt she prayed, fasted, believed God, but death still came, now to add insult to injury her son dies also. There are no details concerning either of the deaths, but I'm almost sure that her conversation with herself and God is, "What is really going on?" Have your ever thought that it can't possibly get any worse than this and then it does. Well that's not just the Widow of Nain, that is also many of us. It was bad enough that her husband dies, but even in that she still has her son. It's bad, but we can keep it "in-house", we can keep it covered up because with the help of her son it still didn't have to go outside of the house. It may be a struggle, but we can make it, but when the son dies that's another story. This death is felt worse than the husband's because not only does she lose the son, but also her last chance to receive any inheritance. With no son, there is no way to claim her inheritance. From worse to worse and from "in-house" and covered to a very public death and situation. Without her son, there is no inheritance and she will now be at the mercy of the public. Has anyone ever been at the mercy of public charity? Along with their charity comes their opinion too. If your there, remember there's always going to be a day after. When the crowds know your business, it's always going to be a day after. When you thought you had that one thing left that would help you keep your dignity and you lost that too, not in private, but very publicly. When you made yourself "satisfied" with losing That as long as you had This and the "This" died too, there's always going to be a day after. I want to encourage someone, you're like the Widow of Nain that lost her only son. You may not have lost your only son, but you lost your only chance, you threw away your big moment and now you feel like you will have to be at the mercy of others for the rest of your life, not so. Jesus is coming to your city. He's about to show up right where you are. You won't have to run him down or search all over for him, he's going to show up just as the entire town thinks that there's going to be a funeral, he's going to show up with your church members and family members watching. Jesus is going to show up, not just with his disciples and much people, but also with compassion. He's coming with pity, inward affection, tender mercy, to be able to be moved, My God!!! Today you have been dealing with those that don't have the ability to be moved about your situation, but there's coming A Day After that you're going to run into the Savior. Jesus couldn't get into the city until the funeral procession came out. I dare somebody to start carrying some things out of your city. Start carrying your last chance out of the city, start carrying whatever you want Jesus to not only touch, but speak to out of the city. What was dead sat up and began to speak, and Jesus delivered him to his mother. I challenge someone to carry those ideas and strategies out of the city, so Jesus can cause them to sit up and speak. Yes, ideas speak, yes, strategies and plans speak and in this season, he's returning them to who birthed them. I call every book, every idea for increase, every unction of invention, every plan back to who birthed it in this season. It will not stay dead and lifeless, it will not be buried, but will take on new life in this season. A new season a new day. Eventually morning has to come. Your season has to change. The Master is going to eventually get to you!!! He's going to eventually get to where you are. Just when it seems as if it's nothing left to do but bury you, he'll show up and turn the funeral into a praise service. There's always going to be a day after because God always visits his people.

Conversation 2

God Knows The Way That I Take

Job²³:⁸ Behold, I go forward, but he is not there; and backward, but I cannot perceive him:

⁹ On the left hand, where he doth work, but I cannot behold him: he hideth himself on the right hand, that I cannot see him:

¹⁰ But he knoweth the way that I take: when he hath tried me, I shall come forth as gold.

This conversation is one we must have with our selves whenever we are feeling anxious, whenever we are feeling like we're lost, whenever we feel like that God doesn't know where we are. When it feels like God is so far away from us. This conversation we must have with ourselves to settle our spirit. Don't get carried away with your feelings in this season. I'll say it again, Don't Get Carried Away With Your Feelings in this season. Feeling will run us into places that God never intended for us to go. Don't get carried away with how your feeling because you will feel a lot of ways a lot of different days. Don't allow your anxiousness to make you make a bad decision or move ahead or out of the will of God. Don't make a move out of your emotions. Emotions is defined as a strong feeling deriving from one's circumstances, mood, or relationships with others. So, it is safe to say that if That would have never happened then I would not be feeling like This. Emotions and feelings are a reaction. Let us not be knocked off course because we didn't get the proper action. Sometimes we must be resolved to be still and wait, but because we run on feelings we are all over the place. We look for answers in people, places, and things and God is not in any of that. Remember that we have a still small voice down on the inside of us that says this is the way, walk ye in it. Some of us are right at that point where we have tried all that we can do. Some are waiting on God to show up in ministry matters, we've prayed, we've fasted, we've kept up our disciplines, some are waiting for God to do something with us even in our business and we have done all we can to do our due diligence. This is where we see Job doing his part. He is pursuing God and most of all he is putting himself in places where he knows were God is. He's definitely in the right place, the place where God is, so after that Job has a resolve in his spirit that He knows the way that I take, he knows right where I am. Most of the time it is in this hard place that we shut down in our pursuit for God. We get weary with chasing what seems to be out of our reach. This is the very time we must begin to put fire back into our pursuit. If the flames are beginning to die out, you have to find a way to fan them so that their intensity may be increased. Yes, God knows the way that I take, but I must put the effort in. Since it's not coming to me then I must be aggressive in this season. God has set you in the right vineyard, he has set you in the right church, he has sent you the right business plan, so you must trust in the fact that he knows right where you are. He knows exactly what I need, he knows right what I've got going on in my life at this very moment. This is a conversation we must have with ourselves from time to time, if not we will be chasing a feeling, we will be chasing people's approval, we will be chasing what other's think and their opinions, we will be chasing people's advice when all we must do is stand still and trust in the sovereignty of God. We must settle our spirits and bind up every anxious spirit that wants to rule us and our emotional realm. The enemy knows that we cannot take feelings of abandonment and loss, so he plays on that to get us off. Let this be the season that we finally mature, we finally grow up and be able to take something. Let this be the season that we can be able to take a No and still stay saved. Can we take a Not Right Now and not leave our church or stay in the church, but stop working in the ministry? Can God or your leader really tell you it's your time, just not your turn yet? Truth be told the word No is the action from God, your leader, your supervisor, your husband, or your parent that many times causes our reactions. You would have never thought about leaving the church until your leader said No. You were not even considering leaving the company you work for and loved until the supervisor said No. One No has got you looking in the help wanted ads. God knows the way that I take and after he has tried me then I will come forth as pure gold. God will use a No to try you. To see what's in your heart. To see if that humility is genuine or false. To be tried means to be thoroughly tested and proved to be good or trustworthy; made to undergo trials or distress. Just like Job, God will use all manner of things to try us. It's not just one thing that will be used to try us, but many things. We don't get to choose. Job was tried in his marriage, in his family, his business, and in his relationships with his friends. It came from many ways. So, it feels like the same with us as times. Before we can catch our breath good, here comes something else. It's in those times where we feel so overwhelmed, we must settle ourselves and say within ourselves, God knows the way that I take.

Conversation 3

Let It Die

Ruth 1:1 Now it came to pass in the days when the judges ruled, that there was a famine in the land. And a certain man of Bethlehemjudah went to sojourn in the country of Moab, he, and his wife, and his two sons.

²And the name of the man was Elimelech, and the name of his wife Naomi, and the name of his two sons Mahlon and Chilion, Ephrathites of Bethlehemjudah. And they came into the country of Moab, and continued there.

³ And Elimelech Naomi's husband died; and she was left, and her two sons.

⁴ And they took them wives of the women of Moab; the name of the one was Orpah, and the name of the other Ruth: and they dwelled there about ten years.

⁵ And Mahlon and Chilion died also both of them; and the woman was left of her two sons and her husband.

⁶ Then she arose with her daughters in law, that she might return from the country of Moab: for she had heard in the country of Moab how that the LORD had visited his people in giving them bread.

⁷ Wherefore she went forth out of the place where she was, and her two daughters in law with her; and they went on the way to return unto the land of Judah.

It's ok to Let It Die. There is a time and season for everything under the heavens. It's a time to live and it's a time to die. As hard as it may seem, somethings just have to die. It's our first inclination to put our everything into what seems to be dying or already dead. We hope, we pray, we even turn down our plate trying to resuscitate it and bring it back to life, but the inevitable must happen. What's worse is we know it and still try and keep it alive anyway. It's ok because while death is working in one thing or situation, life is working in another. To die means to pass away, lose life, expire, to meet one's end, and as much as we hate to say it there be many things in our lives that need to do just that. We need to let the issue die, the relationship die, the attitude die, the bad decisions die because if we let it or them die then we can live. The word of God says that there is a season and a time to every purpose under the heaven. A time to be born and a time to die. The word tells us that It's Ok to Let It Die. There's an opportune time to do everything, a well-chosen or useful time for all things, even death. Yes, even death at the right time can be good, but because we don't want to let some things die we keep stuff alive way to long and miss the season in which we should have let it die. That's where we end up hurting and confused, because now it's three seasons later and we just realized that we should've let it go way back then. We would have been healed up by now had we embraced that season, that appointed occasion to let it die. I'm trying to help somebody. It's your time, your due season, your now, to just let some things die. You did all you could do to salvage the relationship, you did all you could to uproot misunderstanding and confusion. You did your part now let it die. It's ok. Let it die. The Doctor has even come in and pronounced the official time of death and you still in there beating the body. It's dead, it's not coming back. The death of some things around you and concerning you doesn't mean that you are going to die. Just because That dies don't mean that You are going to die. Even if parts of you die that only means that you are about to be rebirthed in some areas. God is about to bring forth the new in you. The word die in this text doesn't just mean that something is going to pass away or expire on its own, it also means to put to death, to kill, to slay. Whatever won't die in this season, that needs to, you better rise up and kill it. It's either you or the relationship, you or the friendship, go ahead and kill it. When God has given you the discernment and insight on the end of the thing or matter don't waste time waiting on it to die, go ahead and kill it. You already know that it ain't going nowhere, it's going to end up pushing you farther away from the things of God, go ahead and kill it. If that situation is already causing your hands to hang down low and be weakened don't wait for that thing to get you even more weak, you better overthrow it now. Don't waste no more time or energy with people, places, or things that you've given your all to and it's still not enough, rise up and help it to die. We need to let this box that we have placed ourselves in die. We can't live because we don't even know who we are anymore. The walls are closing in on us because we can't find a way to get out from under other's expectations and opinions of us. Naomi had a made-up mind to remove from the place that she was in. He daughter's in-law rose up with her, but she was leaving that place. She didn't ask their opinion, nor did she let the fact that they were from Moab box her in and make her stay there. You are never stuck if you let it all die. Many of us are stuck and stagnant because we are trying to keep and save alive what should have been dead a long time ago. Let it pass away, let it expire, let it come to an end. This is a hard but much needed conversation we must have within ourselves. Today I am giving someone permission to let it die. It's ok. Once you let it die you can begin living. We feel breakthrough and breakout in our spirit, but because somethings haven't died yet we can't seem to remove from the place that we are in. Let it die and you will soon see that you can move on from that place that you are in. Look at Naomi here, she ended up in a place that had nothing to do with her decision. That was her husband's decision because of the famine. I'm here to tell you that it doesn't matter how you got there to that place the first thing you going to have to do is let somethings die. We lose hope when all we have to do is let it die. Many of us would rather die ourselves than to let certain things die. Notice I said certain things die, because truth be told its only certain things that we struggle with in this area. We are quick to get the scissors out to cut relationships off and kill certain God ordained friendships and fellowships, but can't get rid of needful things within ourselves. It was never intended for us to die. We have sacrificed self, dreams, visions all because we refused to let our own internal insecurities die. Remember not all of these conversations have something to do with the external things, or beings, but many of these conversations help us to overcome us. We have to speak to and have conversations with our own internal selves. There are parts of us that we must let die. There are attitudes, dispositions, ways of thinking that must die or we will never remove from this place that we are in. I can remember as a young wife there were many ways of thinking that I had to let die. If not, it would have not only destroyed my marriage, but more importantly my own mind. It wasn't that my way of thinking was bad because it was not. Most all young wives' have a traditional way of looking at marriage. I had a predetermined mindset that was very traditional concerning man and woman roles. What I had to realize was that I did not marry a traditional man. The anointing on him made him very peculiar and if I and my marriage were to survive then I had to let my way of thinking die. I had to let the traditional box I was trying to shove him in die. It's Ok to Let It Die. Again, it's more internal than external things and issues that we need to let die. It was somethings in my life that I had to let die in order for me to even write this book. I had to let procrastination, laziness, and please get this last one, being all things to other people, die. Yes, did you think that only bad things have to die? Not so. There are a lot of good things that must die as well if we are going to move out in new dimensions. Let me be transparent here if I may for a moment. There have been some good relationships that I've had to let die in the last season. I truly believe that they were God Ordained, and I never even thought that I'd ever be without them in my life. Some of these relationships had been so near and dear to me for so long I'd forgotten how life was before they came into it. Some much closer than family. Well as the relationships began to be tried, because all real ones will be, I began to see where these relationships where about to go into a season of serious testing and there was nothing it seems, that I could do about it. Well I'm here to tell you that some of those relationships didn't survive the season of testing and died as a result. Now this is where I want to help somebody, some of the relationships survived, but the position that they once held in my life died. I hope I'm helping. Sometimes the position that they held in your life has to die. They are good people, but they just don't occupy the same space in my life anymore. Some folks position in your life must die, their position in your ear, their position in your decisions must die in this season. There be many things that we have poured our blood, sweat, and tears into at one time or another, but the time has come, and the season has changed. It's time to let it die. It's time to go forth out of that place you are in. It's held you hostage long enough. The Message Bible says that Naomi started out from the place she had been living. I encourage someone today to let it die so you can get out of the place you've been residing. You've been residing there in your thoughts, you've been residing there in your actions. Once you let it die you will break free from the place you have been living in. Don't you die trying to let it live, let it die so that you can live. Let it all die so that new life can come, sometimes we must let the old relationships die so that new relationships can come forth. Let the plan die so that the new strategy can come forth. Let It Die.

Conversation 4

At Times There Is Victory In Silence

Proverbs[17:27] He that hath knowledge spareth his words: and a man of understanding is of an excellent spirit.

[28] Even a fool, when he holdeth his peace, is counted wise: and he that shutteth his lips is esteemed a man of understanding.

Everything doesn't need my answer. Somethings may need an answer, but just not necessarily mine. There is much victory and much peace to be had in silence. Free yourself from always having to have an answer. It's very liberating. I'm not God, why do I have to have all the answers. Why must I always speak, why must I always offer my opinion? Self, you know what? Everything doesn't deserve my time, attention, and especially a response from me in this season. I know we live in a world where technology is saying comment, say something, give your input, and what are your thoughts on a wide range of discussions and topics, and because the platform to speak your opinion and mind is right at our fingertips we get caught up and lose sight of the peace that dwells in silence. Men too, but this book is giving insight to women, the enemy is really taking us for a ride thinking that everything deserves a response from us. Many times, we give up hard wrought victories just because we feel we have to say something. We have been walking in a level of discipline where our mouth is concerned for months, we know that God is doing something new in our lives. We begin to see the fruit of discipline, we begin to see the fruit of putting a watch and a guard on our mouths. We then throw away all that deliverance with one response. I've been there and did that to many times to count. I said I will hush, I'm not going to speak on it, I'm not even going to answer. I had been doing good for months and one situation, one tight place comes along and the victory I had been walking in goes out the window. I got tired of that feeling. You know that feeling of dread(conviction) that comes over you as soon as it leaves your mouth. Even when it deemed an answer or response I had to study to be silent in some areas. Yes, I said study, which means to apply one's self to the acquisition of knowledge, as by reading, acquisition or practice, to apply one's self, endeavor, to think deeply, reflect or consider. For many of us women it doesn't come naturally so we have to study to be quiet. Am I saying that there is not a time to speak, no not at all, but we must study to know the difference. There is definitely a time to speak, that's the easy part. We go that part down, but please understand that there is also a time to be quiet. Somebody is not going to like me for this, but let your husband speak, let him answer this time. If you don't have a husband use the same principal with your supervisor, with your mother, with your coworker. The only person that has ALL the answers is God, and we are not him. Let me say it again, I got tired of the feeling, I got tired of knowing what to do and still not being able to do it. I could see it coming like the prudent man in Proverbs 27:12, but because I refused to hide myself and simply passed on I was punished, and boy was I punished. At times, our solace realm (the place where our emotions reside) makes us easy targets. I know as women, we want to be clear, heaven forbid if we are misunderstood in any way, but again somethings just don't need or deserve an answer. For the sake of your peace let it go. That answer or response that you just have to give may end up upsetting your peace for the next six months, it just may throw you in drama or in unnecessary warfare. We must become protectors of our peace at all times. I'm a witness that silence will make you look like you got all the answers. If you can harness your need to be heard and opinionated, it will bring you into a whole new level of wisdom and understanding. Yes, we see a lot as wives, mothers, sisters, and that "keeping it real" friend and yes, it's a lot to be said about a lot of things, but is it necessary. To some of us it has become a sick form of worship, I've been guilty. Some of us just don't even feel right unless we have told someone off or set somebody straight. We somehow don't feel right unless we've given someone a piece of our mind. We are not even going to ask where the other pieces are at. We have forgotten the bible says in Proverbs 29:11 that a fool uttereth all his mind: but a wise man keepeth it in till afterwards. Keep being the one that always has to say it, always have to tell them, always have to show them, or prove something, you will soon tire of the drama and even the responsibility of always having the answer. You didn't know that having all the answers and always having the need to respond to everyone's issues comes with a responsibility? Any leader can tell you that and guess what, it becomes heavy and begins to wear you out. As a leader myself, there are times I will feel the weight of leading others, it comes with the job and I'm graced to do it. Then there are times when I must know, even as a leader, that I don't have everyone's answer. Now if I begin to operate outside of that principle then that's when I begin to carry unnecessary weight. Even to us leaders, it's ok to let folks miss your voice for a season. Let your voice be missed for a while. It will not be the end of the world or your ministries. I'm here to help us we are talking about Victory in Silence. God gives us many ways and many tools to lead his people and the grace to keep you while doing it. Many people are so used to you speaking, having an opinion, or an answer. Let them miss your voice for a season. What do you mean Pastor Von? You are so used to feeding and feeding, imparting and imparting. Some people didn't know that they were even eating until you started feeding them and because of this many have gotten comfortable around you. They have come to your ministries and have gotten encouraged, restored, and you have stood many back up on their feet again. They have gotten so fat off of the telephone prophecies and prayer partner encouragement that they have now began to kick at you and your wisdom as if they came up with all that revelation and understanding that you gave them. Go ahead and let them miss your voice, miss your words of encouragement, and mostly your 24-hour access. I dare someone to let your words be rare in this season. Your words, your advice, counsel, message, report, speech, language, and request be rare in this season. Don't just be tossing it out there anymore. People will begin to disdain anything that is common. In this season let your silence be what shames, be what corrects, and be what rebukes. Get Victory In Silence. I'm not going back in forth in this season, many will have to learn from my silence. Silence is a teacher, it's an instructor. In this season, my words are too precious to be wastefully giving out. Too precious, costly, heavy, fat, rare, prized, and my favorite one to withdraw. Oh my, I almost ran. For your words to stay precious, in order for them to be heavy or carry weight, you must withdraw them at times. Yes, at times you must withdraw them. You must withdraw them from friends that don't appreciate them, children that trample them under their feet, withdraw them from distractors and drainers that you've wasted enough time on. Don't be afraid to withdraw your words in this season. My words of counsel and advice can't mean that much to you if you can carry yourself like I haven't said anything to you. It's time to let your silence convict. If you can walk away from me like I never fed, or sustained you in a past season, well in this next season you are going to have to miss my voice. Sometimes we've had to make hard decisions or take a hard stance and people have tried to act like your words never fed them or were not precious, but let me encourage you that they will miss your voice and your time of intimacy in their lives. Let them miss your voice, your mouth was like an open heaven to them. Let them miss it for a season. I think that you know by now that I am referencing I Samuel 3:1 where the word of the Lord was rare in those days. I believe that that was a part of God's judgement at that time. Why would he or should he speak if you're not going to obey. It's displayed in the life of Eli and Samuel. We have one that couldn't see because he wouldn't obey, Eli didn't just have an eye problem, but he had an ear problem as well. I believe God stopped speaking to him because Eli was not obeying him. We now see Samuel obeying Eli and serving in the temple and God honors him for that by speaking to him. Let your silence convict. I'm not telling you not to build your audiences or your ministries, but for some around you that have started kicking at your wisdom and advice, give them your silence in this season. Don't let anyone drain you with foolishness. Let your silence minister to them that you are too busy for it. It just wasn't Samuel's words that convicted Eli, it was also his silence while working in the temple that shamed him. Let your silence shame. Your "no access" silence in this season will bring shame. God will do something in and for you if you make you voice rare in this season. You can finish some assignments if you make your voice rare in this season. You can walk in more deliverance if you make your voice rare in this season. One more thing, at times your voice should be so rare that others, even those in the temple, may not even recognize it. I'm Getting Victory In Silence, are you up for the challenge?

Conversation 5

I'll Encourage Myself In The Lord

I Samuel 30:1 And it came to pass, when David and his men were come to Ziklag on the third day, that the Amalekites had invaded the south, and Ziklag, and smitten Ziklag, and burned it with fire;

² And had taken the women captives, that were therein: they slew not any, either great or small, but carried them away, and went on their way.

³ So David and his men came to the city, and, behold, it was burned with fire; and their wives, and their sons, and their daughters, were taken captives.

⁴ Then David and the people that were with him lifted up their voice and wept, until they had no more power to weep.

⁵ And David's two wives were taken captives, Ahinoam the Jezreelitess, and Abigail the wife of Nabal the Carmelite.

⁶ And David was greatly distressed; for the people spake of stoning him, because the soul of all the people was grieved, every man for his sons and for his daughters: but David encouraged himself in the LORD his God.

When you find yourself in a place that you have wept until you have no more power to weep you are in a good place.

Let me first say that it's okay to weep until you have no more power to weep. Yes, it ok and perfectly fine and normal. Sometimes we as women try to act like we got it all together and hold it all in like we are ruff and tuff, but the real truth is that we are emotional beings. That is a part of our natural make up as women. We are women, living, breathing, and full of life and emotions. We are not monuments. Lot's wife was turned into a monument because she lingered as she looked back at Sodom and Gomorrah. What has caused you to turn into a monument. Something with no life to it, no emotion to it. What has caused you to become something stationary? No balance in your emotions will cause you to become stationary. We are women, we are not statues. I know that life and society has tried to dictate and tell us otherwise. It has hardened us women more than most men. It has hardened us to the point where many of us refuse to show any emotion, much less cry, but I am here to help free you my sister friend. It's ok to cry. It's ok to cry until we have no more power to weep. If we do so then that means that we have come to our end. So, go ahead and cry and get it all out. In getting it all out you get all of you out and now the Father can begin to work. Now that you have depleted all your natural strength then God's supernatural strength will begin to rise within you. Go ahead and weep. After you weep until you have no more power to weep then you must find a way to encourage yourself in the Lord. Go ahead and have that conversation with yourself. I'll encourage myself in the Lord. People will take you captive, situations will take you captive, issues will take you captive, but when you know how to encourage yourself in the Lord you are never held hostage by what others will or won't do. You might be held captive, but it won't be for long. Encourage yourself on purpose from now on. Thank God for the encouragement of others it is needed and appreciated, but don't get stuck in a place because you are dependent upon how others esteem you. Even if you blow it, even if you milk the cow and kick your own bucket over, that's ok, own it. It did happen, but at the end of the day please know how to encourage yourself. When people rise up against you, when people speak of stoning you, when your whole world has been turned upside down within a few days, encourage yourself. When the enemy and so-called friends spread themselves and lies against you, when they try and strip you of your character and class, when they want to strip and murder your self-esteem and influence, you better know how to encourage yourself. In times of total chaos, just as David was experiencing, you better have this conversation with yourself. Just like David this is not a time to put yourself in nobody else's hands you better begin to speak life to yourself. When everything around you seem to be burned with fire, encourage yourself. We stay in a tough place that God has already ordained that you reign in because we will not encourage ourselves. If you're going to go from Ziklag to the palace (place of reign) then in the middle, you must learn to encourage yourself. We can't be so quick to look for others to do this, some people will withhold encouragement from you on purpose. They may be right there with you and we assume that they are willing to give it. They withhold it because they know that their encouraging words have the potential to push you into another place and that place may very well supersede the place that they themselves are currently in. They don't want you dead just not living more than they are themselves. Just like here in this scripture, they carried them away captive. They didn't want them dead, but they wanted them to be slaves. The Message Bible says, they didn't kill anyone, but drove them like a herd of cattle. People will willingly withhold their encouraging words hoping to drive your expectation, hope, and passion right out of your life like a herd of cattle. Trying to keep it locked up just long enough for you to miss your season and most importantly not become more than them. My Lord, I'm trying to help you here. When you begin to see, everything being herded out of your life you better encourage yourself. Whether someone else does it or not, Encourage Yourself. Remember some really don't want you dead, they just want to make you a slave to them. They want you to be a slave to their way of thinking because they really don't think you need or deserve that level of blessing right now. A slave to them and how they would do a certain thing, not encourage you on purpose because you refuse to be boxed in with their way of thinking or because you won't use their plan or take their advice they hold you a prisoner. Some just don't have the capacity to encourage you. Like David's men they were weeping till they had no more power to weep. They were exhausted with weeping and had nothing left to encourage David with. At the time, they just didn't have the capacity to carry David the way that he needed to be carried. We have all been there. We have all been surrounded by these types of folks at one time or another. Release them and let them go. Forgive them and move on. Drop the charges and save yourself. The capability just was not there for them to encourage David. No malice, no hate, now ill will toward you, just not capable. David didn't get mad either he just did what he had to do, and don't you get mad, no need when you have power and life in your own tongue. Look at how they captured David's wives, their names were listed and we all know names in the bible are many times representative of their character and lives. The one was named Ahinoam the Jezreelitess, which means agreeableness, splendor, grace, to be pleasant or sweet. Woman of God encourage yourself in the Lord, so you won't have to worry about your grace and agreeableness being carried away captive. A woman that can encourage herself in the Lord will be able to maintain her sweetness from the inside and not be needy for something from the outside. Don't walk around here upset with folks, let it come from the inside. The name of the second wife was Abigail, which was Nabal's wife so right off the top she was walking in supernatural wisdom. It was proven that she knew how to handle matters and men. Look at what the enemy wants to capture here. It wants to capture your ability to handle matters wisely. Secondly, her name means source of joy, gladness. It's a dangerous thing to allow your joy and gladness to be captured. These are some things in life that I refuse to put in the hands of someone else. I will encourage myself. I refuse to let it be said that Pastor Von was not walking in grace, sweetness, and agreeableness all because I was waiting around for someone to encourage me, God forbid. I'll take my life into my own hands like Jephthah. I got this, I'll just encourage myself in the Lord. Even in a loving marriage, even when we are surrounded by people that really love and support us, God will still manipulate situations and circumstances to make this lesson concrete within you. He'll allow your husband to forget to encourage you, he'll allow your leader to look over you, just so you can learn how to encourage yourself in the

Lord. The enemy wants to take away your ability to revolutionize your joy. Encourage yourself in the Lord.

Conversation 6

It's Ok To Be Desperate

Luke[8:43] *And a woman having an issue of blood twelve years, which had spent all her living upon physicians, neither could be healed of any,*

[44] *Came behind him, and touched the border of his garment: and immediately her issue of blood stanched.*

[45] *And Jesus said, Who touched me? When all denied, Peter and they that were with him said, Master, the multitude throng thee and press thee, and sayest thou, Who touched me?*

[46] *And Jesus said, Somebody hath touched me: for I perceive that virtue is gone out of me.*

[47] *And when the woman saw that she was not hid, she came trembling, and falling down before him, she declared unto him before all the people for what cause she had touched him, and how she was healed immediately.*

[48] *And he said unto her, Daughter, be of good comfort: thy faith hath made thee whole; go in peace.*

Desperate times calls for desperate measures. Many of us are living and experiencing life that is far from what we dreamed. It is far from our childhood fantasies. For some it has been a whirlwind to say the least. We have not been able to get out of it what most of us have already put in it. We are at a deficit. Many are coming up with the short end of the stick more often times than not. Many of us have had to muster up the strength to get back in the ring one more time, muster up the strength to give it one more go around. We are making a final ultimate effort, giving all, having an urgent need or desire. Many have given up throwing in the towel for this one last chance. This is your chance of a lifetime, this is your final swing at it, and if we don't knock it out the park this time up to bat then we are throwing in the towel for sure. Cuteness has gone out the window as it and desperate don't go well together. We have gotten downright ugly in the face of the enemy to show him and others, and ourselves to that we ain't playing this time. We came ready to fight the good fight of faith, we came ready to tear the enemy's kingdom down. We are not going out without a fight. If it's a fight you want, then it's a fight you'll get. Settle yourself and say It's

Ok To Be Desperate. Many are not enjoying everyday life, we are missing moments because we are locked up and blocked up. If you aspire to be anything in business, anything big in the kingdom you are going to have to be desperate to get it. I can hear the thoughts of many as I delve into this conversation. I can hear the I won't ever do that. I can hear the I'll never act like that. I'd never say that. Well it's a good chance that you won't get to experience the more that God has for you. It's those very thoughts, those ways of thinking, and mind sets that keep you locked in your own prison. Nobody put you there, you willfully went into that cell and closed the cell door behind you. The sad thing is that you have the key, but will you be desperate enough to use it. So, we waste away, throw away our ideas, while our good years pass slowly away. One of the meanings of the word desperate is to make a final ultimate effort, giving all, or having an urgent need or desire. Somebody better make a final ultimate effort to move out in business or ministry. Go ahead and give it your all, its ok. As the women with the issue of blood go ahead and be loosed. You can't get loosed if you are not desperate. Many are still stuck full of potential because we can't find a way to be desperate. I know for many of us strong women that have been carrying the whole load for many years this is strange and uncharted territory. Many of us are in a now or never season. If we miss the troubling of the water this season we may not get the opportunity again. It takes desperation to capture seasons. It took desperation for the woman with the issue of blood to capture her healing and deliverance. The bible says that she had a running issue for twelve years, it also says that she spent all she had. What's your recipe for desperation. The woman had a series of things that happened to her. It was her recipe for desperation. I will ask again, what's the recipe for your desperation. A series of events have to happen to you before you become desperate. If you have no needs and everything is in its proper place in your life, if you have enough money, or your children are model students, I can almost guarantee you are not desperate. There is simply no need for desperation in your life, but if you have a running issue in your life, if you are paying out more than what's coming in, if you are being taken advantage of an being overlooked, if you try and try and it still gets worse, then that's a good recipe for desperation. It says that this woman had spent all, have you spent all? Have you spent all on your job, have you spent all in your marriage, have you spent all in your ministry? If so I dare you to get desperate enough to reach for your own business. Have you spent all? Have you spent all on your wayward children, I dare you to get desperate enough to sow a seed, desperate enough to go on a fast. Don't give up just because you've spent all, this is the time for desperation to kick in, don't be satisfied with that, you got something else to give and it's called desperation. To be desperate you have to be able to be vulnerable. The world and life say that if your vulnerable that you will be trampled and ran over. It has always dictated to us that we must always be strong and stay on the offense. To be honest vulnerability is not a trait that has been shown or displayed to us as women. We fight devils, we are not vulnerable. To get what you want your going to have to take a chance and open yourself up, you may be susceptible to physical or emotional attacks or harm, but that's the chance you just have to take. The woman here suffered many things of many physicians and I give her much credit because even in that she found a way to try again. Don't be afraid to be vulnerable because you have suffered many things of many people. Don't be so quick to think that if you try you are going to end up in a worse position then what you started out with. In this season, you must be desperate enough to touch the Master. I will be desperate enough to touch him from behind. He's not looking at me, so he doesn't even know that I need something from him. Let the chips fall where they may, but I'm going to touch the Master. I don't care how many people are trying to get to something from him, I'm still going to touch him. I don't care what people think of me, I'm getting desperate. I don't even care if I'm in the way, I am desperate enough to trouble the Master on his way to someone else's miracle. You have pushed and supported many, but in this season, know that your hearts desires are important enough to get the Master's attention. I command somebody to get desperate enough to come out of hiding. That's right come out of hiding, come out of that nice neat box that you've been keeping You in. I had to come out of hiding just to write this book. I had to get desperate in order to write my thoughts and insights not knowing how it would be received. Even as a leader everyone is not going to agree with you, some may not even think you have anything to say or offer, but I had to take a chance that there was someone that wanted to hear what I had to say. I had to become vulnerable and expose myself to possible rejection in order to birth this book out. I had to fight through the crowd of fears, people's faces, and insecurities. You have to fight against people fighting against your audacity. They have every chance to do the same things that you did, but were not desperate enough to take the chance, but hate you because you did. I'm here to help somebody because all you need is a word from the Master asking who touched me, after that I didn't hear no one or see no one but Jesus. I had to be vulnerable enough to admit, yes Master I need you. Get desperate enough to take a chance on the Master. What do have to lose? I dare you Woman of God to get desperate enough to leap. I've been saying for a while now, that this is going to be the year that I Leap. The year that I break free from Me, the year that I become desperate enough to reach for different.

Conversation 7

I Will Thrive Where I'm Planted

Jeremiah[29:4] *Thus saith the LORD of hosts, the God of Israel, unto all that are carried away captives, whom I have caused to be carried away from Jerusalem unto Babylon;*

[5] *Build ye houses, and dwell in them; and plant gardens, and eat the fruit of them;*

[6] *Take ye wives, and beget sons and daughters; and take wives for your sons, and give your daughters to husbands, that they may bear sons and daughters; that ye may be increased there, and not diminished.*

[7] *And seek the peace of the city whither I have caused you to be carried away captives, and pray unto the LORD for it: for in the peace thereof shall ye have peace.*

[8] *For thus saith the LORD of hosts, the God of Israel; Let not your prophets and your diviners, that be in the midst of you, deceive you, neither hearken to your dreams which ye cause to be dreamed.*

[9] *For they prophesy falsely unto you in my name: I have not sent them, saith the LORD.*

¹⁰ For thus saith the LORD, That after seventy years be accomplished at Babylon I will visit you, and perform my good word toward you, in causing you to return to this place.

When It seems as if you have been carried away captive in some areas, when it seems as if you have gone from a full place, a place where you were prospering, a place that was flowing like water in one season, and now you find yourself in total confusion. You don't understand this place, you definitely don't know how you have been carried away to this place, it's in this place that you have to make up in your mind that you are going to have to thrive in the place that you are planted. Tell you, tell yourself right now, go ahead and have a conversation with yourself that I will thrive where I'm planted. The word thrive, means to grow or develop well or vigorously, to prosper, be fortunate or successful, flourish. I want to encourage you today to go ahead and thrive where you are planted. Yes, yes in this place. I know right now you're in a place that you've been carried away to. You didn't get to this place because you wanted to go or be there, but you've been carried away to this place. Not just that, but you are captive. You can't get out of it just because you want to.

You can't pray your way out, you can't fast your way out of this place and please understand why. It's because it's God ordained, it's God allowed. Everything we go through is not because of the enemy. A lot of what we go through has been manipulated by the Master. Stop trying to get out of what He has placed you in the midst of. God knows what it's going to take to get certain things out of us. We see here his people were in bondage and he allowed them to stay there until certain things were accomplished in their lives. He commanded them to build houses and dwell in them, plant gardens, and eat the fruit of them. He wanted them to thrive even in a place of captivity. He wanted them to build houses because they were not leaving that place no time soon. Stop wanting to get out of places fast and quickly. God has something that he wants us to get out of these uncomfortable places and if we move too fast we increase our chances of not getting it. In that place keep on planting, keep on sowing. Don't shut yourself up or in because you're in a place of captivity, continue to thrive in that place. He still wants us to plant our goodness, our kindness, our longsuffering even in that place. We don't get let off the hook because we are in a tight place or and uncomfortable place. We must still plant. We are planting because God says we must be able to eat the fruit of that place. You get no harvest if you don't plant. It's a hard place, a strange place, a place of confusion, but God still wants us to bring forth fruit in that place. We must grow and develop vigorously there. Many of us have been in places that we were not able to eat the fruit of because we refused to plant. We shut up our bowels of compassion because we were feeling some type of way because God allowed us to be in certain places. He allowed us to be carried away captive and made us dwell there and the last thing on our minds was thriving and growing, much less getting a harvest from that place. We spent the time in those places upset and angry at God and people grumbling and complaining. There's nothing worse than being in a place for a time and season and not getting the harvest out of that place, meaning we didn't learn a thing. We didn't get the revelation, the understanding, the other level of anointing and we simply wasted the season. I encourage someone today, don't waste another season. God wants fruit to be added to you while in this place of confusion, don't waste the season. God then goes on further to say, get married in this place and have children. Since you are going to be here until the time appointed is up, go ahead and reproduce in that place. Yes, reproduce in that place of captivity. This is foreign to many because this place makes us steer away from intimacy. We are so upset with God that we stop all intimacy with the father. We don't pray, we don't read, and there is no way to reproduce without intimacy. It's the same in the spiritual as it is in the natural. If you're going to birth anything you must become intimate. Multiply in the place that you've been carried away to. Go ahead and have this conversation with yourself. It may not be a comfortable place, and everything is not set up the way that I had hoped or prayed, but I'm here now and since I'm here I will find a way to thrive where I am planted. I don't have to be planted in the best of conditions to thrive. I don't have to be planted in my favorite spot to thrive. I know that you are in captivity, but you will be increased there. Find a way to be multiplied there. Multiply in your homes, in your marriage, in your careers, and spiritually. Multiply. Increase there and don't lessen, don't pare off, or fall off. I prophecy that you won't fall off in this season, you won't become small or little, but that you will increase, be enlarged, and excel! Find a way to live in peace there. You be at peace in this place. Seek peace, don't cause trouble, don't try and pull people into your captivity. Just like in Babylon it is plenty of people that are living there and loving it, but for you it is a place of captivity. My God today. We have all been in a place like that. We are agitated and frustrated in a certain place, but when we look over at our neighbor they are satisfied. So please understand that there be many living in places that you are held captive in. You've been the one carried away captive not them. So, in this season you find a way to live peacefully amongst them. It's your warfare, your season of testing, not theirs. It's yours, not your neighbor, not your husband, but yours. Find a way to thrive there, grow there, and develop there. Sometimes in our confusion we lose our footing and begin to grasp at certain people, places, and things trying to catch ourselves in order to keep from falling. This is where we can mistakenly drag others into this place with us. Please don't drag your church into this, don't drag your prayer partner into this, it's your place of captivity. Please don't drag your pastor into this, your husband into this, or even the lack of encouragement from a trusted source into this, it's a set up for You, now Thrive. It's there in this place of confusion, this place we are confounded in, and it seems as if we are fading in this place, that if not careful, we will begin to reach for what's really not there. We must be careful in this place that we don't begin to hear what we really didn't hear. Oh My. That we don't allow the voice in our own head to be mistaken for the voice of God just because we refuse to thrive where we are planted. After we have been in a place for an extended amount of time we, if not careful will begin to put words in the mouth of God just because we want to get out of where He allowed us to be carried away to. I'm helping somebody here. Remember, I said earlier that there are people living in loving the place that you are being held captive in. Don't let these people conjure up prophetic words for you in this season just because they know that you are in captivity and they are not. Some are not in captivity because God is not trying to get out of them what he's trying to get out of you. Don't let your itching ears be quick to hear a word when you already know that God wants fruit to be added to you in spite of this place that you're in. People that are in the midst of you, those that are closest and nearest to you can deceive you the quickest because they know and can see that you are in captivity. They love you, they don't want to see you in a hard place, so everyone is coming up with prophecies and everyone is dreaming dreams, can I encourage you today to just Thrive. At the appointed time, God is going to visit you. After you've been multiplied and increased in that place. After you've learned how to dwell peaceably in that place. God knows exactly what he has in mind concerning you and that hard place will produce the fruit that he is looking for out of your life. You've got to Find a way to Thrive where your Planted. I want God's good word to be performed in my life. In this season, I will show the enemy, and most of all myself that I can thrive where I'm planted.

NOTES

_____

_____

_____

_____

_____

_____

_____

_____

_____

_____

_____

_____

NOTES

About The Author

Pastor Von, as she is affectionately known, is an awesome Woman of God. She is the Pastor of More Sure Word Church under the Senior Leadership of her husband Apostle Daniel L. Akins, to whom she has been married for over twenty years. Although Pastor Von was already doing the work of a Pastor she was officially ordained in 2004. She is not a pastor in name or title only, but a true co-laborer deep in the trenches of ministry.

Pastor Von exemplifies a Proverbs 31 woman, with a Naomi anointing as she has been appointed by God to help lead this generation of women into another place in him. She has been a mentor and confidant to many pastor's wives and other women of God in leadership. Pastor Von encourages women to be empowered, healed, set-free, and delivered through the Word of God and one on one mentoring conversations. It was from these intimate life changing exchanges that Conversations with Pastor Von was birthed. She also mothers many in and outside of the four walls of her church. Pastor Von also founded God's Gems Women's Ministry in 2012. This women's ministry has reached many and hosts an annual conference yearly.

Pastor Vonyett S. Akins was born in Milford, Delaware, but has made Warner Robins, Georgia her home. She is Nina to Ty'Nae, Kamari, Shyzarah, Vaiya, Carson, Tyra Rose, Kai, Kaiden, Kingston, Tyrell Jr., and Kannon. Pastor Von is also a proud Mary Kay Consultant.

FOR ADDITIONAL INFORMATION ON SEMINARS AND SCHEDULING SPEAKING ENGAGEMENTS OR FOR MORE INFORMATION ON

GOD'S GEMS PUBLISHING

CONTACT:

PASTOR VONYETT S. AKINS

P.O. BOX 2612

WARNER ROBINS, GA 31099

PHONE: 478-324-3511

EMAIL: vonyettakins@gmail.com

WEBSITE: WWW.CONVERSATIONSWITHPASTORVON.ORG